Name   W9-AVB-266

Date

To parents Have your child trace the path with his or her finger, then with a pencil. For extra practice, have your child continue to trace the path with different colored pencils. Give your child plenty of encouragement and praise your child at the completion of each exercise.

Draw a line from the arrow (➜) to the star (★) by following the path.

Draw a line from the arrow (➜) to the star (★) by following the path.

2 | A Stroll in the City

Draw a line from the arrow (➜) to the star (★) by following the path.

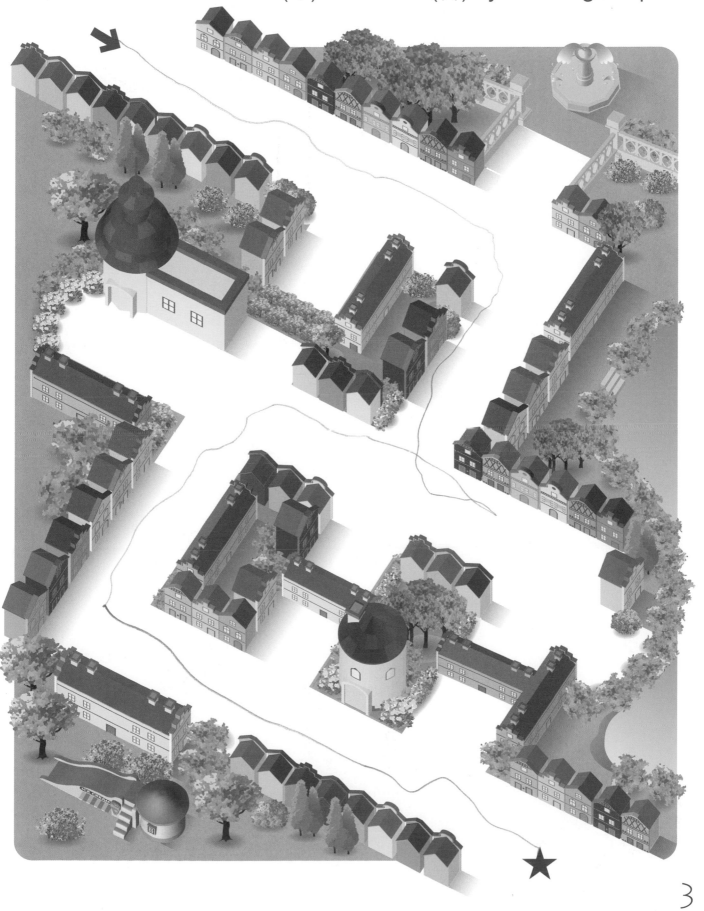

3

Draw a line from the arrow (➜) to the star (★) by following the path.

3 Fun at the Farm

Name

Date

Draw a line from the arrow (➡) to the star (★) by following the path.

Draw a line from the arrow (➡) to the star (★)
by following the path.

4 The Dark Forest

Draw a line from the arrow (➡) to the star (★) by following the path.

Name

Date

7

Draw a line from the arrow (➜) to the star (★) by following the path.

Friends at the Pond

Name

Date

Draw a line from the arrow (➡) to the star (★) by following the path.

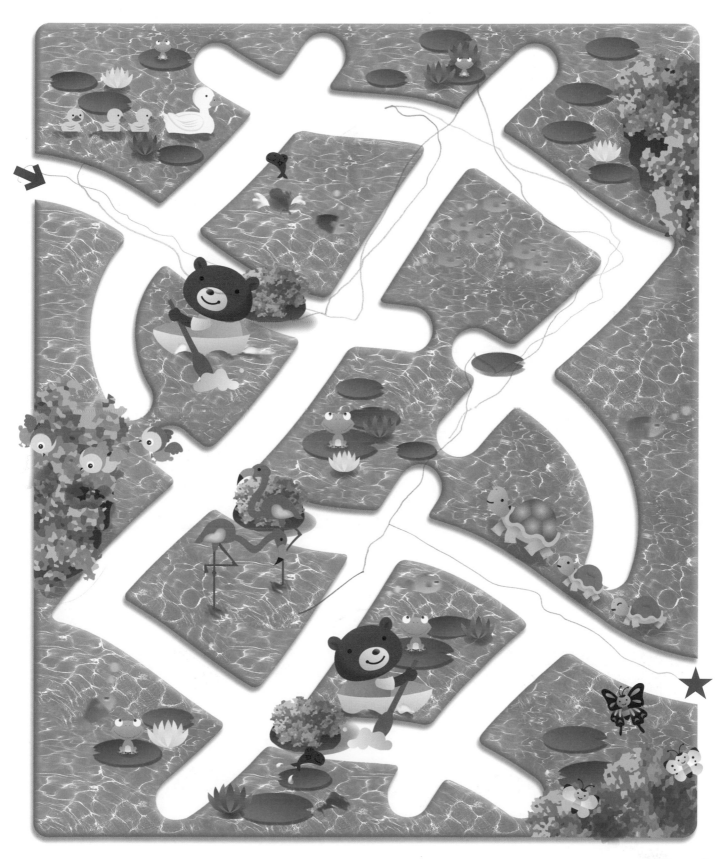

Draw a line from the arrow (➜) to the star (★)
by following the path.

Autumn in the Park

Draw a line from the arrow (➡) to the star (★) by following the path.

Draw a line from the arrow (➡) to the star (★)
by following the path.

7 Vegetable Patch

Name

Date

Draw a line from the arrow (➡) to the star (★) by following the path.

13

Draw a line from the arrow (➡) to the star (★) by following the path.

8

Strawberry Patch

Name

Date

Draw a line from the arrow (➡) to the star (★) by following the path.

Draw a line from the arrow (➡) to the star (★) by following the path.

Ready, Set, Race!

Draw a line from the arrow (➜) to the star (★) by following the path.

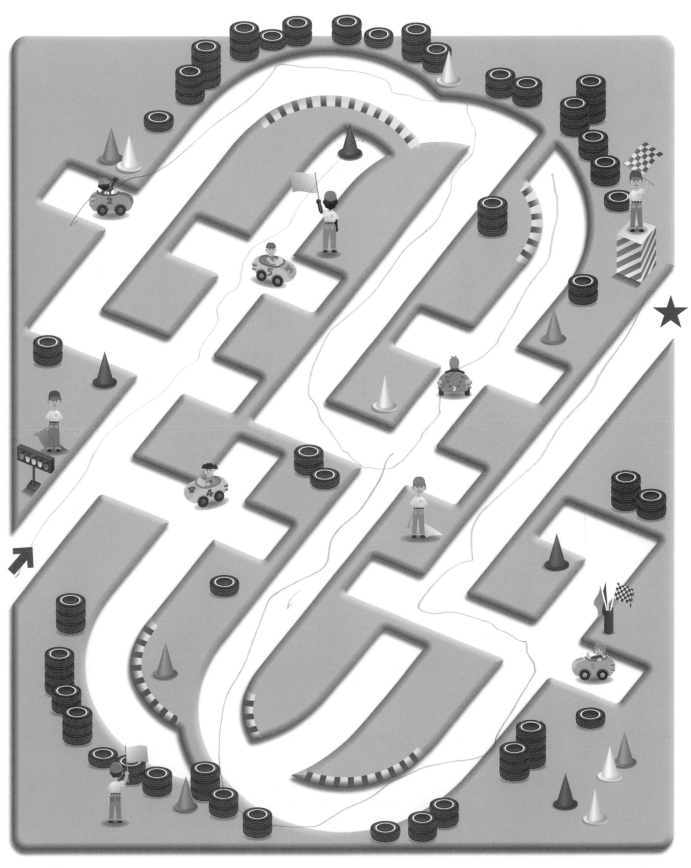

Draw a line from the arrow (➜) to the star (★) by following the path.

City Streets

Name

Date

Draw a line from the arrow (→) to the star (★) by following the path.

Draw a line from the arrow (→) to the star (★) by following the path.

11 Dog Walking

Draw a line from the arrow (➜) to the star (★) by following the path.

21

Draw a line from the arrow (➡) to the star (★)
by following the path.

12 Spring in the City

Draw a line from the arrow (➡) to the star (★) by following the path.

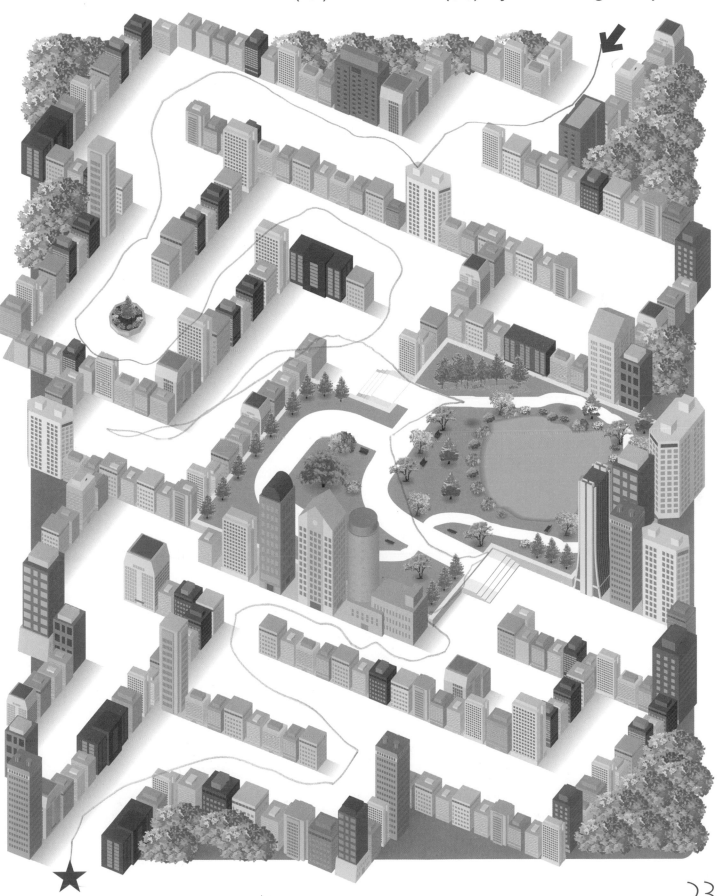

23

Draw a line from the arrow (➡) to the star (★)
by following the path.

13 Tiny House Town

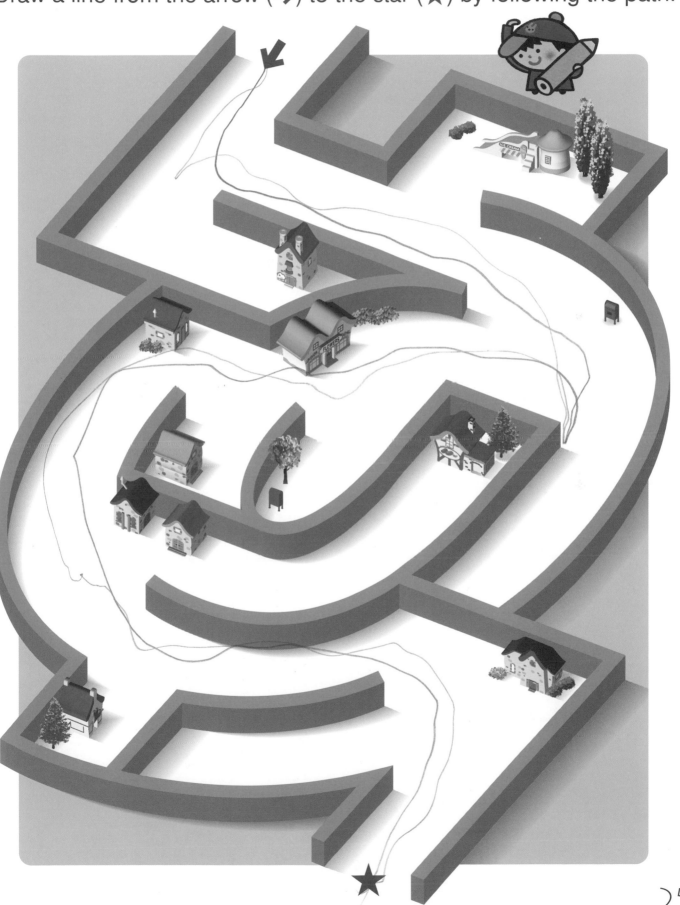

Name

Date

Draw a line from the arrow (➜) to the star (★) by following the path.

Draw a line from the arrow (→) to the star (★)
by following the path.

14 Little Lost Sheep

Name

Date

Draw a line from the arrow (➡) to the star (★) by following the path.

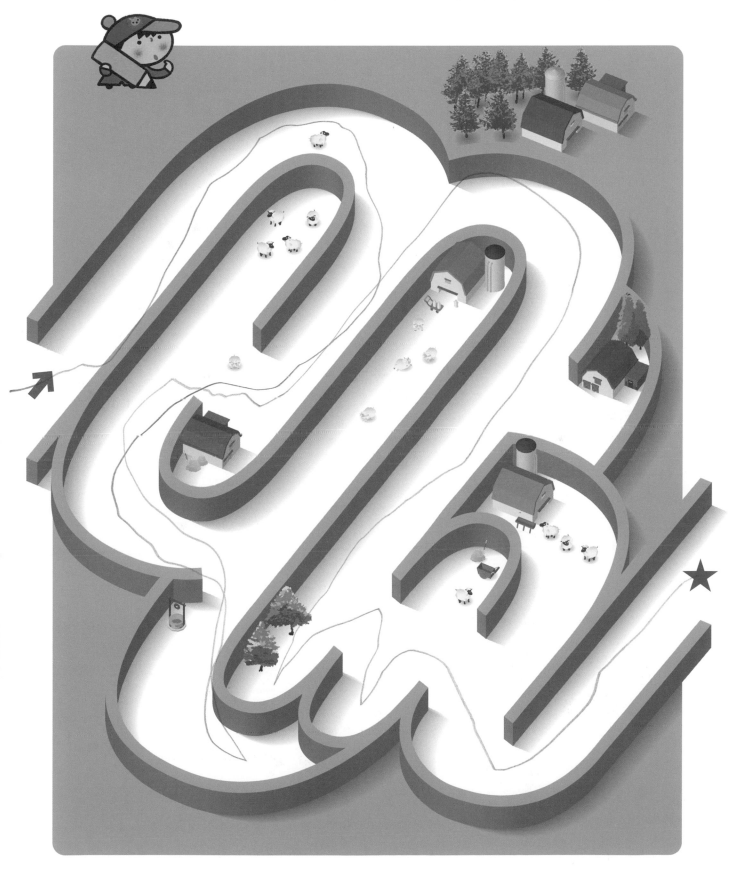

Draw a line from the arrow (➡) to the star (★)
by following the path.

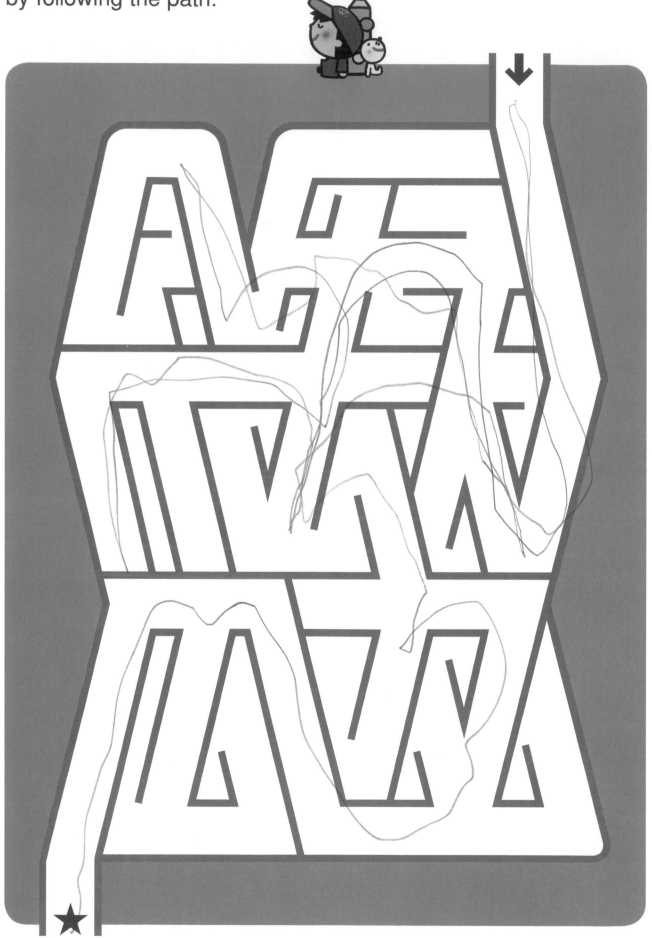

15 Autumn Trees

Name

Date

Draw a line from the arrow (➡) to the star (★) by following the path.

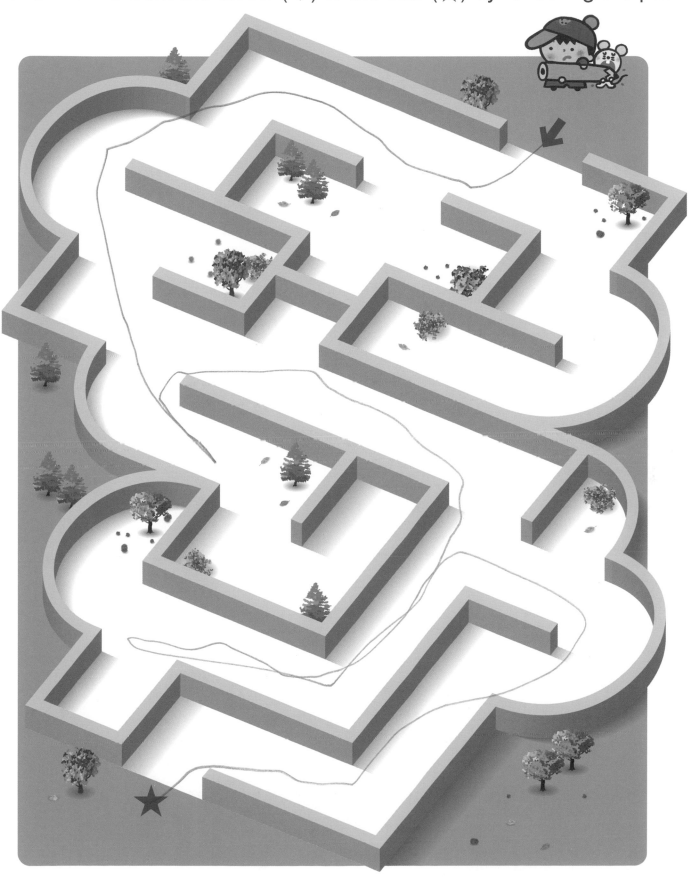

29

Draw a line from the arrow (➔) to the star (★)
by following the path.

Winding Waterway

Draw a line from the arrow (→) to the star (★) by following the path.

Draw a line from the arrow (➜) to the star (★) by following the path.

Autumn Leaves

Draw a line from the arrow (→) to the star (★) by following the path.

Draw a line from the arrow (➔) to the star (★)
by following the path.

34

18 Picking Pumpkins and Cabbage

Name

Date

Draw a line from the arrow (➜) to the star (★) by following the path.

35

Draw a line from the arrow (→) to the star (★)
by following the path.

Let's Pick Some Strawberries!

Name

Date

Draw a line from the arrow (➡) to the star (★) by following the path.

Draw a line from the arrow (→) to the star (★) by following the path.

20 Around the Racetrack Curves

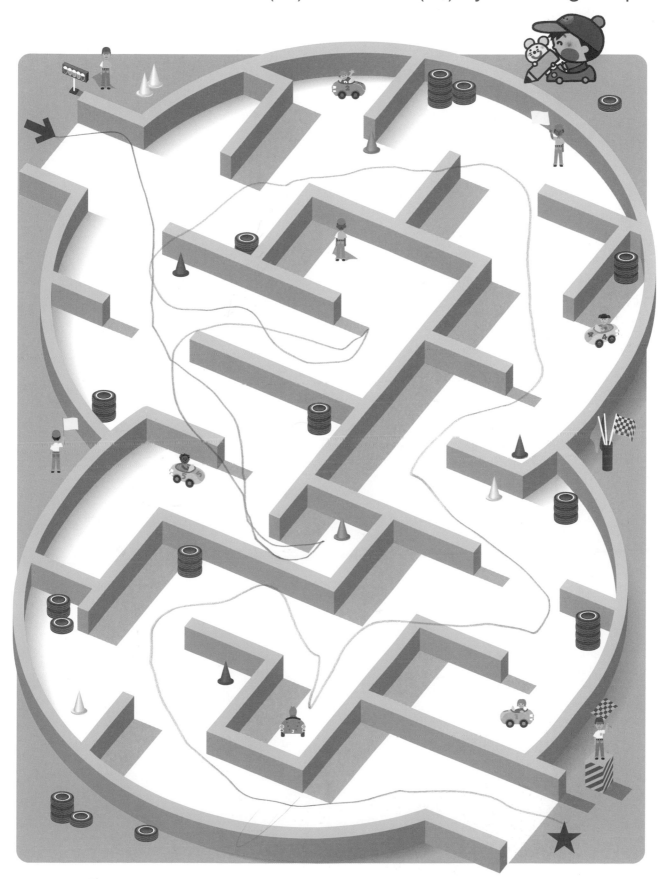

Draw a line from the arrow (→) to the star (★) by following the path.

Draw a line from the arrow (➡) to the star (★)
by following the path.

Turning Corners Through Town

Name

Date

Draw a line from the arrow (➡) to the star (★) by following the path.

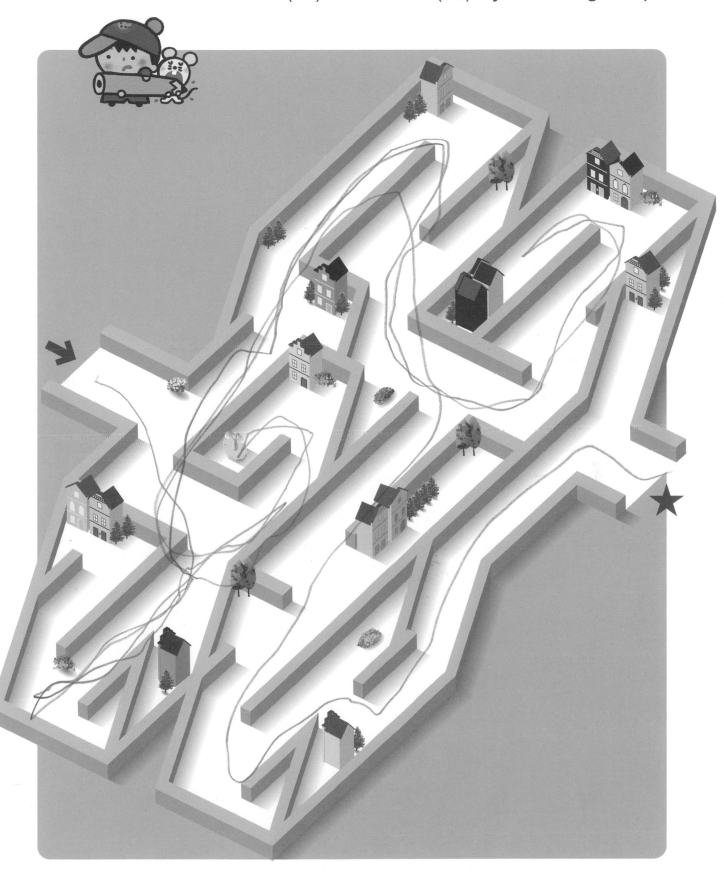

Draw a line from the arrow (➡) to the star (★) by following the path.

Name

Date

Draw a line from the arrow (➡) to the star (★) by following the path.

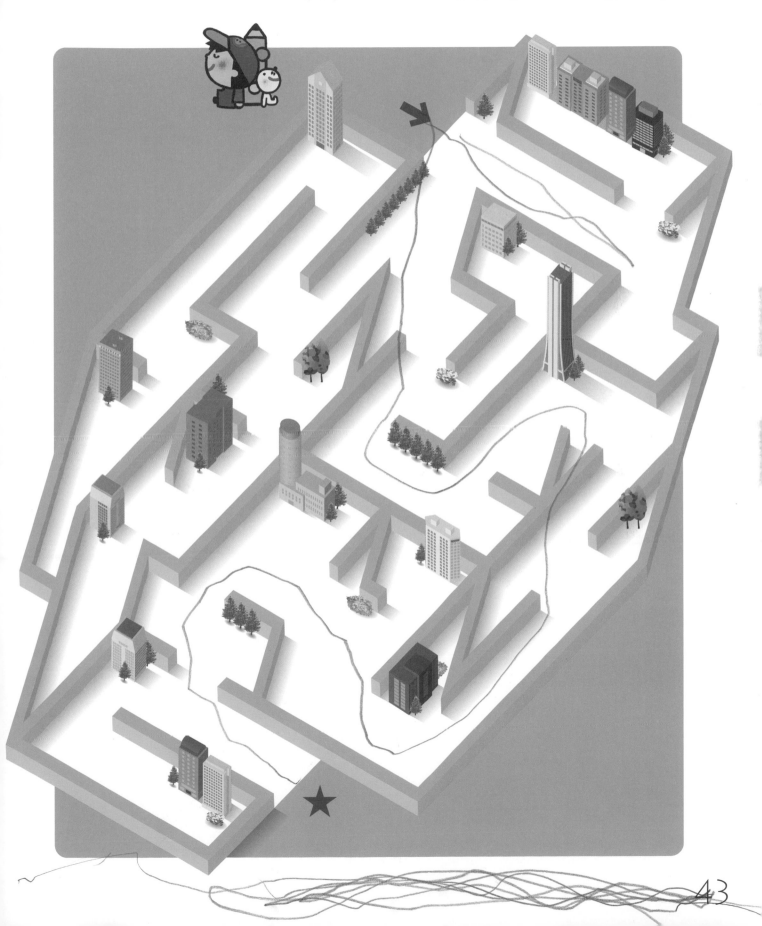

Draw a line from the arrow (➡) to the star (★) by following the path.

23 Finding Flowers on the Way

Name

Date

Draw a line from the arrow (➜) to the star (★) by following the path.

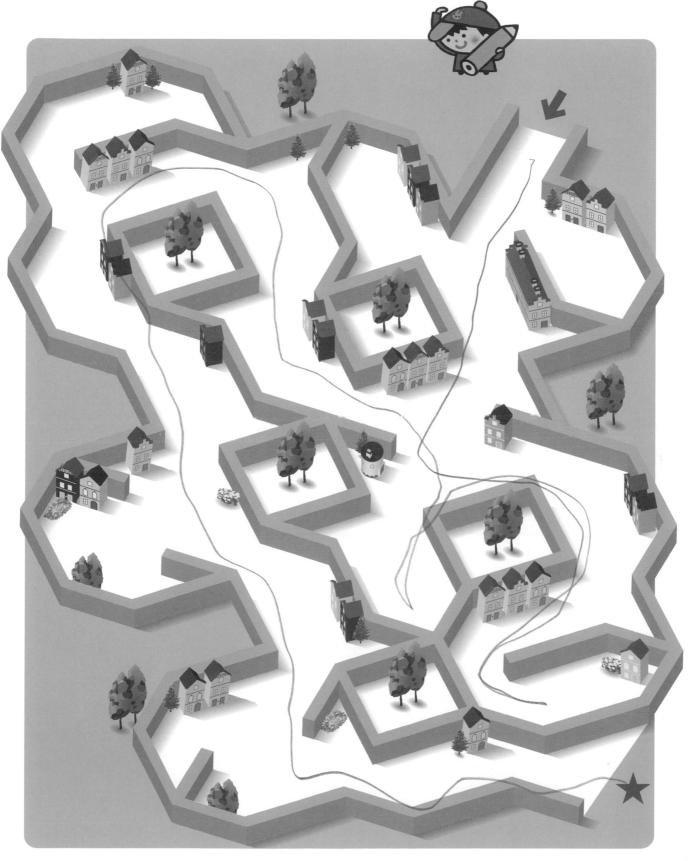

Draw a line from the arrow (➡) to the star (★) by following the path.

24 Old MacDonald's Sheep

Name

Date

Draw a line from the arrow (➡) to the star (★) by following the path.

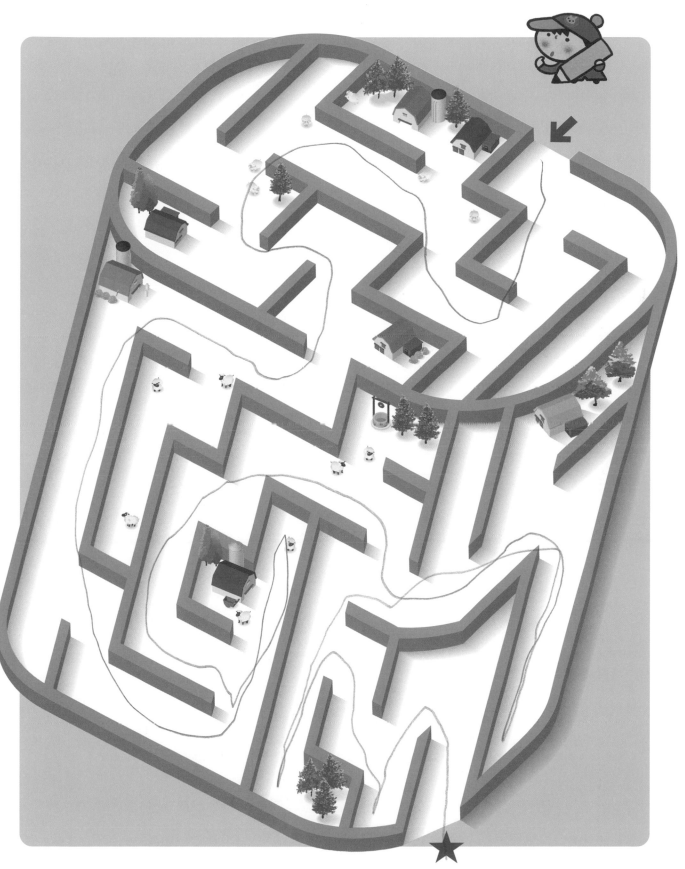

Draw a line from the arrow (➡) to the star (★)
by following the path.

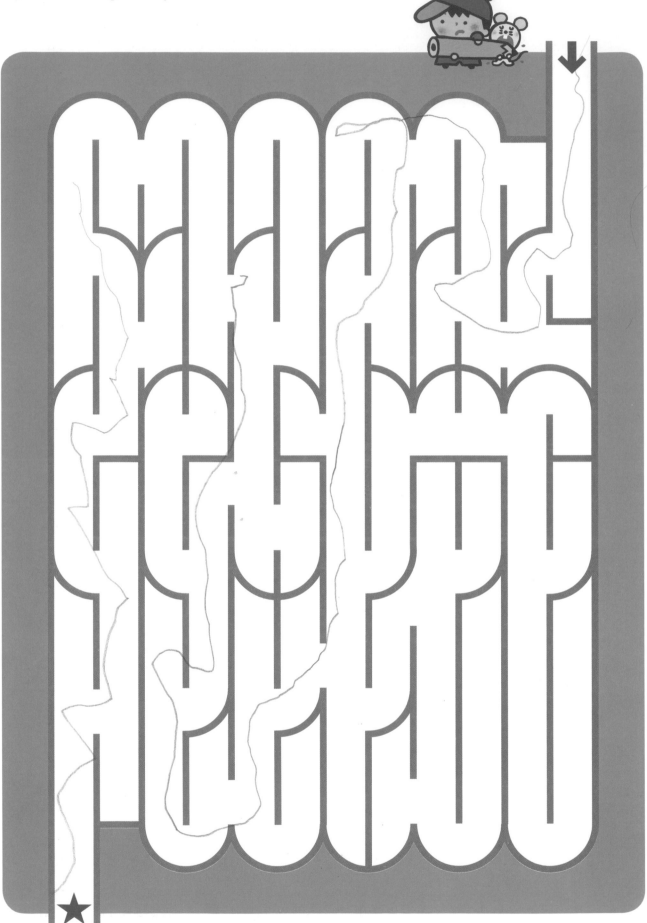

25 Far Away Village

Draw a line from the arrow (➡) to the star (★) by following the path.

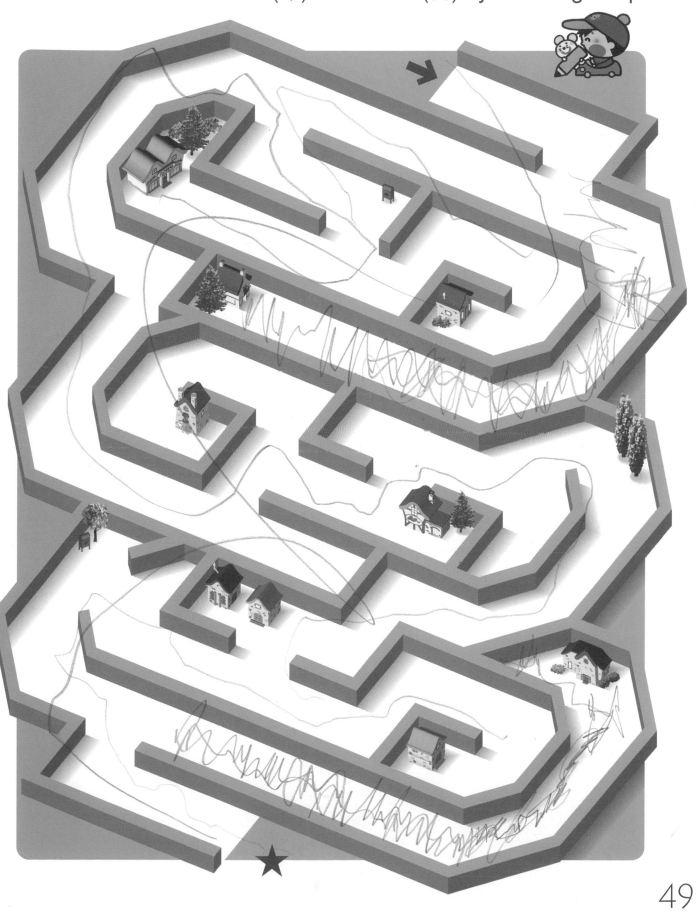

Draw a line from the arrow (➜) to the star (★)
by following the path.

26 Buzzing by Buildings

Name

Date

Draw a line from the arrow (➡) to the star (★) by following the path.

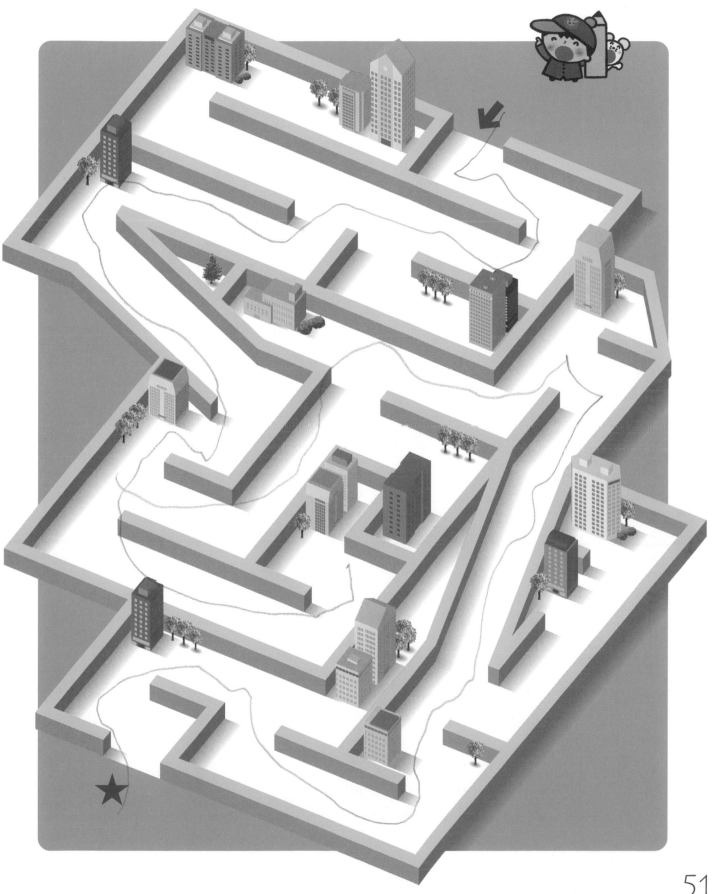

Draw a line from the arrow (→) to the star (★)
by following the path.

Autumn Forest Trail

Draw a line from the arrow (➜) to the star (★) by following the path.

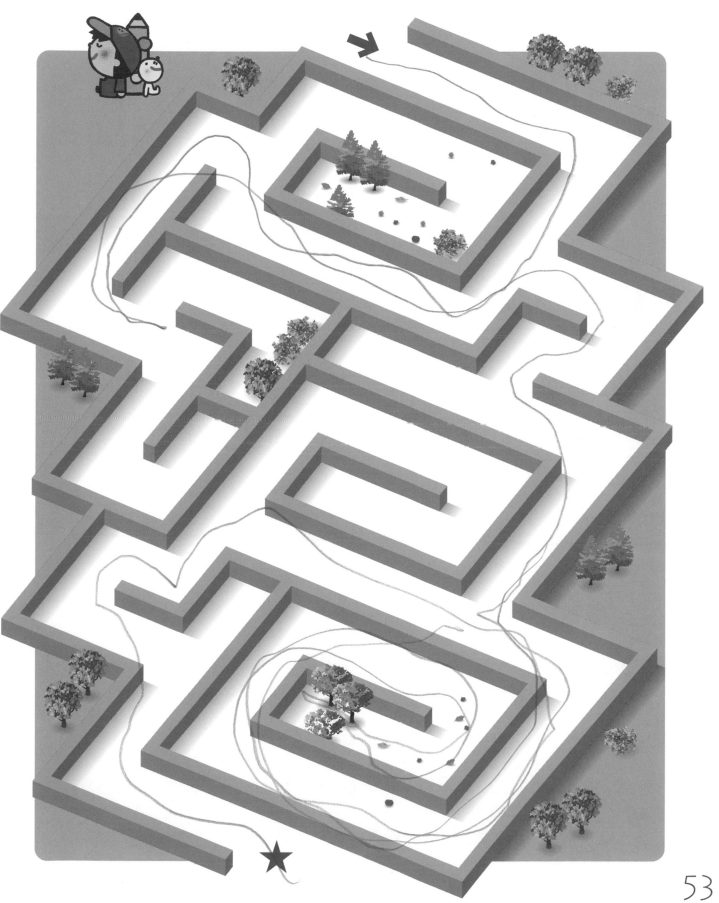

Draw a line from the arrow (➡) to the star (★)
by following the path.

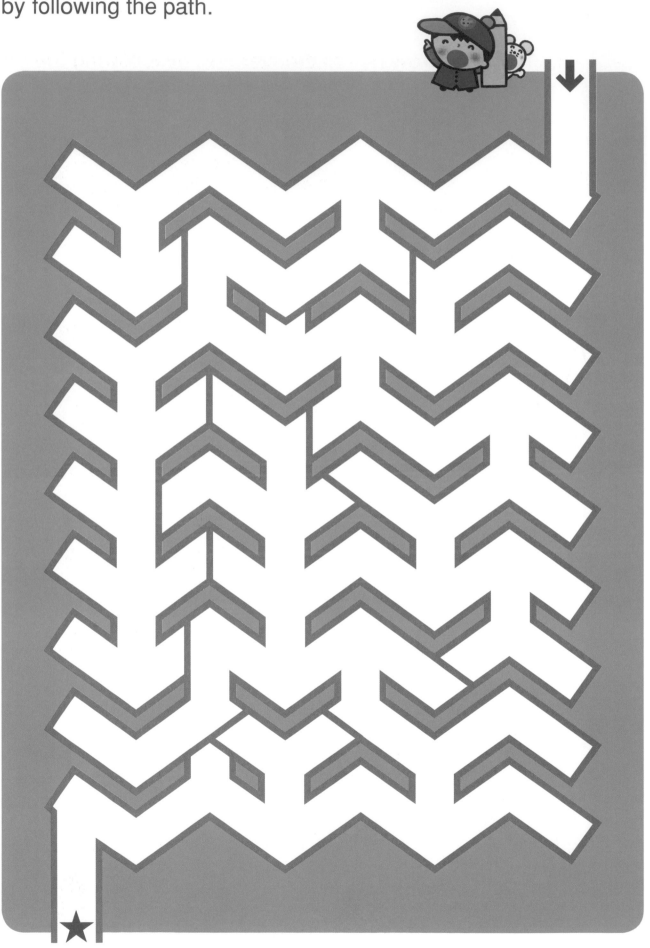

54

28 Paddling the Pond

Name

Date

Draw a line from the arrow (→) to the star (★) by following the path.

Draw a line from the arrow (➜) to the star (★)
by following the path.

29 | Baker

Name

Date

To parents
Starting with this page, the maze patterns are different from others in the book. Mazes on even-numbered pages have narrower paths and are more challenging. When your child completes each exercise, praise him or her.

Draw a line from the arrow (➜) to the star (★) by following the path.

Draw a line from the arrow (➜) to the star (★) by following the path.

Name

Date

Draw a line from the arrow (→) to the star (★) by following the path.

Draw a line from the arrow (➡) to the star (★) by following the path.

Name

Date

Draw a line from the arrow (➡) to the star (★) by following the path.

Draw a line from the arrow (➜) to the star (★) by following the path.

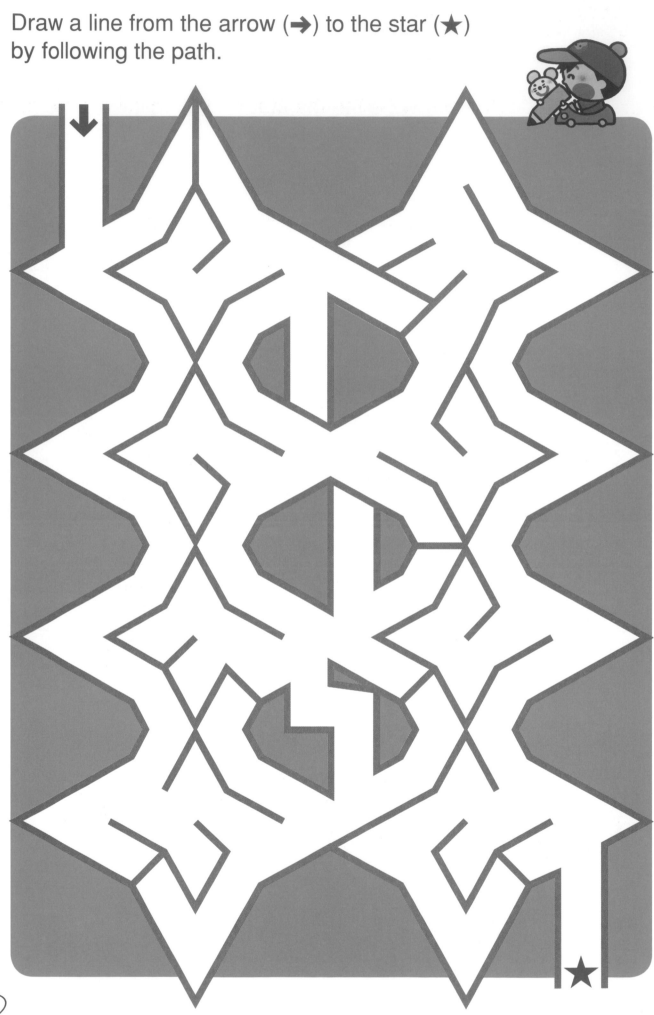

Draw a line from the arrow (➡) to the star (★) by following the path.

Draw a line from the arrow (➡) to the star (★)
by following the path.

Bear Playing Golf

Name

Date

Draw a line from the arrow (➡) to the star (★) by following the path.

Draw a line from the arrow (➜) to the star (★)
by following the path.

34 Fox Playing Soccer

Name

Date

Draw a line from the arrow (➜) to the star (★) by following the path.

67

Draw a line from the arrow (➡) to the star (★)
by following the path.

Draw a line from the arrow (→) to the star (★) by following the path.

Draw a line from the arrow (➜) to the star (★) by following the path.

Name

Date

Draw a line from the arrow (➜) to the star (★) by following the path.

Draw a line from the arrow (➡) to the star (★) by following the path.

Name

Date

Draw a line from the arrow (➜) to the star (★) by following the path.

Draw a line from the arrow (➡) to the star (★)
by following the path.

Name

Date

Draw a line from the arrow (➜) to the star (★) by following the path.

75

Draw a line from the arrow (➜) to the star (★) by following the path.

Name

Date

Draw a line from the arrow (➡) to the star (★) by following the path.

Challenge! 1

To parents
The maze pattern on this page is different from others in the book. Do the practice along with your child if he or she has difficulty. Make sure that the line is vertical or horizontal, not diagonal.

Draw a line from the arrow (→) to the star (★), connecting only tulips (🌷).

78

Name

Date

Draw a line from the arrow (➜) to the star (★) by following the path.

Challenge! 2

To parents
The maze pattern on this page is different from others in the book. Do the practice along with your child if he or she has difficulty. Make sure that the line is vertical or horizontal, not diagonal.

Draw a line from the arrow (➜) to the star (★), connecting only rabbits (🐰).

80

KUM⊙N

Certificate of Achievement

is hereby congratulated on completing

My First Book of Mazes

Presented on _____ , 20 ____

_____
Parent or Guardian